Introduction
– the purpose of this book

A nice early Mk3 on a summer evening drive.

The purpose of this book is simple: to remove some of the worries and difficulties associated with choosing and buying a Mk3 MX-5. For ease of reference, the various names associated with Mazda's small sports car since its inception – Eunos Roadster, Miata, MX-5 and Roadster – will simply be grouped as 'MX-5' as that is the classification in the United Kingdom. The MX-5 discussed in this book is the Mk3 model, known internally by Mazda as the NC, with the first model being the NC1, and the following face-lifts being the NC2 and NC3. Where NC is used in this book it encompasses all models, whereas if NC1, 2 or 3 are used the information will pertain only to that model.

The NC model was such a radical departure from the cars that went before, it's amazing it was so good. The model range and special editions were so well planned there isn't a good car or a bad car to point out, they are all good in their own way. Writing the section on undesirable features was a challenge as, in the author's opinion, the Mk3 is fairly devoid of them!

This book will help you to sift through the adverts, auctions and car dealers and choose the car (and seller) that you want to deal with. It will provide the necessary information to help you choose the model that suits you, and find the best example of that model for your budget. We will discuss the benefits of buying a cheaper example that needs work, versus one in better condition that can be enjoyed from day one, as well as the merits of buying privately, from a dealer or at auction.

Resilience is key to finding the perfect car. You may travel miles to see a car that promises the world, yet, on arrival, is more of a scrapyard escapee than the driving partner you dreamt of. Keep the faith, don't get discouraged, and, most

3

A late model
Mk3.5 interior.

importantly, don't be tempted to settle, you will always regret it – you know the right car will come along the second you buy the wrong car.

For readers outside the UK

This book is applicable to a world market, although the models described here are mainly UK examples. The NC was intended to be a worldwide model; however, there are small variations between specifications for other markets. A good example of this is the engine choices available: buyers in the UK and Europe were offered a choice of a 1.8- or 2.0-litre engines, but US customers were only offered the 2.0-litre. The 2.0-litre in the USA also apparently produced more horsepower, but

The stylish PRHT roof.

The Essential Buyer's Guide

MAZDA

MX-5 MIATA

Mk3, 3.5 & 3.75 models, 2005-2015

Your marque expert:
Oliver Wild

VELOCE PUBLISHING
THE PUBLISHER OF FINE AUTOMOTIVE BOOKS

www.veloce.co.uk

First published in May 2022 by Veloce Publishing Limited, Veloce House, Parkway Farm Business Park, Middle Farm Way, Poundbury, Dorchester DT1 3AR, England. Tel +44 (0)1305 260068 / Fax 01305 250479 / e-mail info@veloce.co.uk / web www.veloce.co.uk or www.velocebooks.com.
ISBN: 978-1-787117-54-9; UPC: 6-36847-01754-5.

This is a rare example of the 'appearance package,' fitted to an NC1 model. The package included a front lip spoiler, more aggressive side skirts, and a rear bumper lip.

Stunning forged wheels fitted to Z-Sport models.

this could be down to an error in documentation. While power outputs between territories do change due to mapping and mechanical differences, the NC was built as a worldwide model with regards to its mechanical and emissions features, and there seems little reason for the USA cars to produce more power. Unless specifically stated, specifications listed in this book relate to UK/European models.

Thanks
I'd like to thank my wife, Sarah, whose constant help and support makes my day-to-day work possible, and enables me to write when I get the chance. Not to mention my many fantastic customers, whose cars feature in my books at times.
     And now on to the book. Let's get your new car chosen!

Contents

The Essential Buyer's Guide™ currency
At the time of publication a BG unit of currency "●" equals approximately £1.00/US$1.25/Euro 1.19. Please adjust to suit current exchange rates using Sterling as the base rate.

1 Is it the right car for you?

– marriage guidance

Controls

The Mk3 MX-5 has light steering with good feedback, a light clutch, and a direct yet smooth gear change. The pedals are well spaced, close enough to heel and toe, and wide enough to suit any footwear.

This steering wheel has been upgraded, but the picture shows the clear layout of controls.

Basic model range

The NC range consists only of two-seater, two-door sports cars, all rear-wheel drive. The main differences between the core models of the range are:

• Two body styles: a soft top (ragtop) convertible, or an electrical folding hardtop – the PRHT (Power Retractable Hard Top).
• Two engines: the 1.8- or 2.0-litre.
• Three gearboxes: five-speed manual, six-speed manual or six-speed automatic.

This series was designated NC by Mazda (but usually known as the 'Mk3' by owners) and was sold from 2006-2008. The first face-lift was called NC2 (or Mk3.5), sold from December 2008-2013, and the second face-lift was known as the NC3 (Mk3.75), which ran from 2013 to the model's termination in 2015.

A comfortable place to consume miles!

Will it fit in your garage?

Being a small sports car, the MX-5 should fit in most standard garages, but read below for the facts and figures.

Length	4000mm (157.5in) (soft top)
	4020mm (158.3in) (PRHT)
Width	1720mm (67.7in)
Height	1240mm (48.8in) (soft top)
	1255mm (49.4in) (PRHT)

More details are provided in chapter 17 Vital statistics.

Usability

The car is ideal as a daily driver, weekend car, commuter, or track car. Generally the car rides very smoothly – a complete departure from the sports cars of old; now rough roads can be tackled without one's fillings shaking free! This is in part due to the advanced and much improved suspension design, but also the very forgiving shock absorber and spring packages Mazda chose. Drivers wanting to regularly push their car, especially on track, may benefit from a suspension upgrade, although this will almost certainly increase ride harshness on the road.

Parts availability

Parts are readily available, see chapter 16 for details of suppliers and useful contacts.

There are plenty of handy cubby holes.

Interior space

Legroom is around 1090mm (43in), which is generous for the type of car. Most drivers will find the NC spacious and comfortable, and the seat and steering wheel adjustments can cater for most shapes and sizes.

Luggage space is a generous 150 litres. Notably, neither the soft top or PRHT roof fold into the boot (trunk) area, so the space you see in the boot is yours to use. Further storage is available in the roof cavity inside the car when the roof is up.

Owners are treated to cubby spaces galore: one in the boot to accommodate the jack, tools and other odd small items; one between the seats in the rear of the centre console (which also hides the fuel flap release); and, when the seats are slid or tilted forwards, two hidden doors reveal a pair of generous cubbies on the soft

A good-sized boot with tie down straps for your belongings.

An easy to access engine for maintenance.

top, while the PHRT model has one cubby here, and access to the electronics for the PRHT roof and Bose amplifier (if fitted). The cup holder in the centre section doubles up as useful storage in NC1 models; in NC2/3 models the cup holder section includes a removable divider to turn it in to a dedicated and useful storage space. All NC models have a cup holder in each front door card, as well as a particularly large glovebox. There is a smaller cubby by the driver's knee on the door side of the dashboard for small items, and NC2/3 cars had a useful luggage net at the base of each door card to store small flat items. Where fitted, the luggage net on the passenger side of the transmission tunnel can be useful, but is easily damaged. Finally, PRHT cars came with a small tray mounted to the wind deflector. It is of dubious use for much beyond a pen and would eject it's contents if the wind deflector were ever folded.

Running costs
Servicing is recommended every 12,500 miles. The fuel economy is roughly 35mpg or 6.72L/100km in realistic daily driving. Parts costs are low, and garage labour costs are average.

Investment potential
As Mk3s are still a comparatively new car they are likely to depreciate further before, perhaps, climbing in value as future classics.

Weak points

There could be engine issues if the car is not maintained or cared for properly: most notably, the early cars can develop an oil-burning habit. While this may be due to various factors, poor servicing likely contributes. Unfortunately, if left unchecked, a low oil level can result in the oil pump sucking up air instead of oil, and the resulting knocking bottom end will necessitate a replacement, or at least rebuilt, engine.

Rust can be an issue, but is much less of a problem than on previous models, and rarely expensive to have resolved.

The suspension on NC1 cars sometimes feels a bit high and floaty. This can be improved by fitting NC2/3 shocks and springs, or lowering springs from a reputable brand such as Eibach. For the ultimate handling improvement a set of purpose-built 'coilover' shocks will provide an excellent improvement to handling, although at the cost of some comfort.

New suspension time! Tired old suspension can be changed in one hit with a comprehensive coilover kit such as this one. Although these are aimed more at track use than for the road, and comfort level may be compromised, most kits have adjustable damping which will help.

Strong points

The Mk3s are tough, enjoyable and fun cars. Maintenance costs and overall ownership costs are low, and they are still priced keenly in the market. The excellent roof system completes a very desirable package.

Alternatives

BMW Z4, Porsche Boxster, Honda S2000.

2 Cost considerations
– affordable, or a money pit?

Most costs are similar across the NC range for things such as servicing, insurance, fuel usage etc, and do not differ much between the earliest 1.8 base model and the latest special edition 2.0. However, the condition of the car will greatly affect your ownership experience and subsequent costs. A well loved and cared for earlier or lower specification car could be a far better investment than a similarly priced 'better' car (later/higher specification), as by the time refurbishment costs are taken into account the 'cheap' car may be anything but. Of course, you may view the refurbishment as part of the fun of ownership, but make sure you go into the deal with your eyes open, and don't be swayed by shiny features!

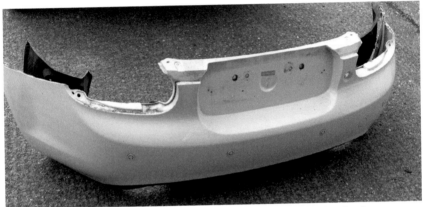

Body panels are available new and used. Used parts are obviously cheaper.

Servicing costs
General (non-main dealer) service ●x150
Oil filter ●x10
Air filter ●x10
Oil ●x40
Brake pads ●x50 for front and rear
Brake discs ●x100 for front and rear
Tyres ●x50-100 each

Body parts
Hardtop ●x500-600
Bonnet (hood) (used) ●x50
Front wings (used) ●x50
NC1 front bumper ●x50
NC2/3 front bumper ●x300
NC1 rear bumper ●x50
NC2/3 rear bumper ●x150
NC1 headlights ●x50

Repair panels such as this rear wing allow for economic rust repairs.

NC2/3 headlights ●x150
Bootlid (trunk lid) ●x50
Leather seats ●x200
Cloth seats ●x50
Wheels ●x50-75 each

Other parts
Standard shock absorber and spring ●x100
Set of four 'coil overs' ●x600
Standard exhaust back box (aftermarket)
  ●x150
Stainless exhaust back box ●x250
Aftermarket stereo with satnav full kit ●x400

Here, a rear shock absorber is being prepared to have a lowering spring fitted; the many parts of the shock unit are shown.

Left: There were many types of wheel; these later items are a nice upgrade to an early car.

A full stainless exhaust system: an upgrade and cost saving over an original replacement.

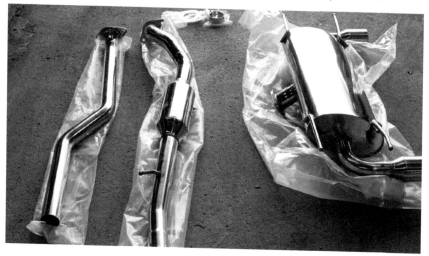

3 Living with an MX-5 Mk3
– will you get along together?

There is no 'typical' MX-5 owner, and the car's appeal is very wide. The Mk3 in particular has an incredibly diverse group of owners of all ages, and is used for all sorts of different jobs. There are those who use the MX-5 as their only car, some for whom it is a fun car for the weekend, or those who use it as a stripped-out track car. Some owners pile hundreds of miles a week on the car; others use it maybe once or twice a month. The common theme here, though, is that, no matter how you use your car, it will take it, and give back in joy in a way I've known no other car to do.

From a practicality point of view – a decent boot, lots of cubby holes, plenty of room to pack luggage – it's a tourer's dream. Of course, this makes the car just as good for the weekly shop (yes, you can get it all in!) as long journeys to work.

The interior is comfortable in the extreme. A classic roadster, with legs outstretched seating position, very comfortable seats, and as many mod cons as you would expect in a sports car. All have electric windows, mirrors, power steering, ABS and a good stereo: features that were not to be taken for granted just one generation of MX-5 ago. Higher specification cars got leather trim, traction control, Bose stereos, climate control, heated seats, and satellite navigation! The heater is

The ideal drive for days out in the countryside.

The Mk3 has great luggage capacity, though it's questionable how useful this tiny shelf mounted to the wind deflector is!

excellent: with the roof up it has the cabin warm (and windows cleared) in minutes, and even with the roof down it keeps off the cold in sub-zero temperatures, especially when used in conjunction with heated seats and the excellent built-in wind deflector.

The car's wide track and long travel suspension may initially have been designed to give a compliant ride with good handling, which it delivers in abundance, but it also makes it a driver's car to match any other. A bit of suspension lowering and stiffening, a few tweaks here and there, and the car can hold its own on track with much more serious cars, or simply be a great back road blaster.

Driving dynamics are generally very good, early cars benefit from a slight lowering, but the standard ride height is handy if you live in an area with poor roads. Visibility is fairly good, although when the hood is up it can obscure some of the side view at junctions. The solution is simple: get it down! The hood is dropped as simply as opening a single catch and throwing it backwards. Raising the hood is no harder than reaching back and pulling it up, then latching at the front – a matter of seconds – and you don't even need to leave the seat. For the PRHT most of this is done electrically, and nearly as quickly!

Around town the car is utterly without quirks, you could be driving a small shopping car for how easy the Mk3 is to thread through traffic. No need to worry about the engine overheating, this is a thoroughly modern car. On a motorway the car will cruise at 70mph with ease, and be able to make progress where needed, while offering a comfortable and reasonably quiet place to enjoy the stereo and eat up the miles. But it is on the back roads the car comes alive: working the engine up to its red line, enjoying the smooth and precise gear change and the lively direct steering. The exhaust as standard is a touch muted for some, but equally loved for its quietness by others. A simple back box swap will add noise if required, and the Duratec/MZR engine does have a nice exhaust note.

The 1.8-litre is a good steady performer, the 2.0-litre, especially in six-speed form, loves to rev. The gearboxes are a delight, steering is direct, while brakes are sure-footed and not prone to fade.

Later cars received face-lifts inside and out, though all cosmetic parts can be

You might enjoy working on your own car ...

... or even tuning for performance.

Most would agree the last of the line Mk3.75s were stunning-looking cars.

swapped across to make your perfect car. There was also some suspension tuning on later cars, which became slightly lower and stiffer for a much improved ride, and the engine was strengthened with a forged bottom end. The early cars, however, have a purity about them, they are not mechanically weak and should be enjoyed fully. All the engines have chain-driven camshafts, so there's no cambelt to worry about, and the gearboxes and differentials are strong. Rust is overplayed: the cars do need care and attention, but if looked after they will not rust away in front of your eyes.

4 Relative values
– which model for you?

Mk3 values are simple: the newer the car, the more valuable. Mileage, condition, accident history, etc, all affect value, of course, but in general a late Mk3.75 will be worth more than an early Mk3. Percentage values given for the models below are relative to a standard Mk3.75 in good condition.

Specification-wise, the higher spec cars are worth more, but the difference is negligible. Generally PRHT and soft top values are pretty level, it is more a matter of personal taste.

Automatics appeal to a smaller market, but value is not noticeably lower, helped by the excellent gearbox.

Mk3 NC1 soft top and PRHT (2005-2008)
1.8- or 2.0-litre engines, UK market five- or six-speed manual gearboxes (six-speed only available on 2.0, and powershift auto available in other markets). 30-55%

The NC1 or Mk3 represents the start of the new generation of cars.

18

Mk3.5 NC2 soft top and PRHT (2009-2012)

1.8- or 2.0-litre engines with strengthened bottom ends, five- or six-speed manual gearboxes (six-speed only on 2.0), and powershift six-speed automatic.   80-90%

The NC2 or Mk3.5 was the first face-lift with improved headlights and updated bumpers/side skirts.

Mk3.75 NC3 soft top and PRHT (2013-2015)

1.8- and 2.0-litre engines, five- or six-speed manual gearboxes (six-speed only on 2.0) and powershift six-speed automatic.   100%

The NC3 or Mk3.75 was a short-lived final update, bringing a slightly changed front end.

Special editions based on one of the production models usually sit slightly higher in terms of value. They represented good value when new, often giving a lot of extras for minimal extra cost, so they make good secondhand buys, too.

The PRHT folding hardtop is an excellent practical solution to the soft top or hardtop debate.

The Mk3 range offered some great special editions, but the Z-Sport was a particular highlight.

5 Before you view
– be well informed

To avoid a wasted journey, and the disappointment of finding that the car does not match your expectations, it will help if you're very clear about what questions you want to ask before you pick up the telephone. Some of these points might appear basic, but when you're excited about the prospect of buying your dream MX-5, it's amazing how some of the most obvious things slip the mind. Also check the values of the model you are looking at in current car magazines, which give both a price guide and auction results.

Where is the car?
Is it going to be worth travelling to the next county/state, or even across a border? A locally advertised car, although it may not sound very interesting, can add to your knowledge for very little effort, so make a visit – it might even be in better condition than expected.

Dealer or private sale?
Establish early on if the car is being sold by its owner or by a trader. A private owner should have all the history, so don't be afraid to ask detailed questions. A dealer may have more limited knowledge of a car's history, but should have some documentation. A dealer may offer a warranty/guarantee (ask for a printed copy) and finance.

Cost of collection and delivery?
A dealer may well be used to quoting for delivery by car transporter. A private owner may agree to meet you halfway, but only agree to this after you have seen the car at the vendor's address to validate the documents. Conversely, you could meet halfway and agree the sale but insist on meeting at the vendor's address for the handover.

View – when and where?
It is always preferable to view at the vendor's home or business premises. In the case of a private sale, the car's documentation should tally with the vendor's name and address. Arrange to view only in daylight and avoid a wet day. Most cars look better in poor light or when wet.

Reason for sale?
Do make it one of the first questions. Why is the car being sold and how long has it been with the current owner? How many previous owners?

Condition (body/chassis/interior/mechanicals)
Ask for an honest appraisal of the car's condition. Ask specifically about some of the check items described in chapter 7.

All original specification
An original equipment car is invariably of higher value than a customised version.

What lies beneath! You won't always see these horrors at first; however, a deep inspection will reveal them.

Matching data/legal ownership

Do VIN/chassis, engine numbers and licence plate match the official registration document? Is the owner's name and address recorded in the official registration documents?

For those countries that require an annual test of roadworthiness, does the car have a document showing it complies? (An MOT certificate in the UK, which can be verified on 0845 600 5977 or online at gov.uk/check-mot-status)

If a smog/emissions certificate is mandatory, does the car have one?

If required, does the car carry a current road fund licence/licence plate tag?

Does the vendor own the car outright? Money might be owed to a finance company or bank: the car could even be stolen. Several organisations will supply the data on ownership, based on the car's licence plate number, for a fee. Such companies can often also tell you whether the car has been 'written-off' by an insurance company. In the UK these organisations can supply vehicle data:

DVLA 0844 453 0118
HPI 0113 222 2010
AA 0800 056 8040
RAC 0330 159 0364

Most modern cars have the chassis number visible in the windscreen like this.

Other countries will have similar organisations.

E10 fuel
E10 fuel, with its higher ethanol content, is considered safe to use for the Mk3 MX-5 NC series.

Insurance
Check with your existing insurer before setting out, your current policy might not cover you to drive the car if you do purchase it.

How you can pay
A cheque/check will take several days to clear and the seller may prefer to sell to a cash buyer. A banker's draft (a cheque issued by a bank) is a good as cash, but safer, so contact your own bank and become familiar with the formalities that are necessary to obtain one. These days it is most common to arrange a bank transfer once you are happy with the car.

Buying at auction?
If the intention is to buy at auction see chapter 10 for further advice.

Professional vehicle check (mechanical examination)
There are often marque/model specialists who will undertake professional examination of a vehicle on your behalf. Owners' clubs will be able to put you in touch with such specialists.

Other organisations that will carry out a general professional check in the UK are:

AA 0800 056 8040 / www.theaa.com/vehicle-inspection (motoring organisation with vehicle inspectors)

RAC 0330 159 0720 / www.rac.co.uk/buying-a-car/vehicle-inspections (motoring organisation with vehicle inspectors).

Other countries will have similar organisations.

Before you rush out of the door, gather together a few items that will help as you work your way around the car:

This book
Reading glasses (if you need them for close work)
Magnet (not powerful, a fridge magnet is ideal)
Torch
Probe (a small screwdriver works very well)
Overalls
Mirror on a stick
Digital camera or smartphone
A friend, preferably a knowledgeable enthusiast

This book is designed to be your guide at every step, so take it along and use the check boxes to help you assess each area of the car you're interested in. Don't be afraid to let the seller see you using it.

Take your reading glasses if you need them to read documents and make close up inspections.

A magnet will help you check if the car is full of filler, or has fibreglass panels. Use the magnet to sample bodywork areas all around the car, but be careful not to damage the paintwork. Expect to find a little filler here and there, but not whole panels. There's nothing wrong with fibreglass panels, but a purist might want the car to be as original as possible.

A torch with fresh batteries will be useful for peering into the wheelarches and under the car.

A small screwdriver can be used – with care – as a probe, particularly in the wheelarches and on the underside. With this you should be able to check an area of severe corrosion, but be careful – if it's really bad the screwdriver might go right through the metal!

Be prepared to get dirty. Take along a pair of overalls, if you have them. Fixing a mirror at an angle on the end of a stick may seem odd, but you'll probably need it to check the condition of the underside of the car. It will also help you to peer into some of the important crevices. You can also use it, together with the torch, along the underside of the sills and on the floor.

If you have the use of a digital camera, take it along so that later you can study some areas of the car more closely. Take a picture of any part of the car that causes you concern, and seek a friend's opinion.

Ideally, have a friend or knowledgeable enthusiast accompany you: a second opinion is always valuable.

7 Fifteen minute evaluation
– walk away or stay?

So, you have shortlisted some cars, talked on the phone with the sellers, and have set a day to go and look at them. You will notice I wrote 'cars' as opposed to 'car.' If you can, do try to set up a few viewings in a day, for one thing it's more efficient, but it also gives you a good escape plan from bad cars, bad sellers, or even a great car that makes every single fibre of your being shout "Buy, buy, buy!"

Stop. Buying the first car you see is rarely a good move. (The author is, however, reminded of one occasion when he was looking for a car well out of his comfort zone and walked away from the first car he saw, only to realise after a year or so of hunting that it really was one of the best out there.) With a car as abundant as an MX-5 you will have no problem finding another if the ideal car sells before you can get back to do a deal.

The first thing to consider is whether the seller is a dealer or a private individual? They could be a dealer masquerading as a private seller to avoid legal responsibilities once the car is sold. A private owner will know the history of the car, whereas a dealer would not, so ask some pertinent questions, and take a look at the surroundings: are they what you would expect? This can give you a clue as to whether the seller is honest. You could be handing over a substantial amount of money to someone you have never met, so trust is key.

If the seller is a dealer, are they a dealer in MX-5s? That's probably a good

MX-5s can sometimes be found on dealer forecourts. Buying from a dealer has the benefit of additional guarantees, compared to a private sale. You may get a bargain buying from a general dealer, but specialist dealers will likely have more knowledge about these cars.

Colour mismatches are rarely this obvious. But we are focusing on the panel gap here.

thing, as they will hopefully value their reputation and know the cars well enough to avoid retailing a bad example. If the seller is a private individual, do the surroundings suggest a well-looked after car?

As you walk towards the car you can often see more in the first few seconds than in the next 15 minutes of more detailed checking. Look underneath the car, are there signs of oil leaks on the ground? A quick glance down the sides of the car and the front and rear will reveal stone chips, scratches, ripples, or poor panel gaps. A Mk3 should be arrow straight and have excellent panel gaps. A rough

Follow the gap between bumper and wing; it is clearly not straight. Investigate further.

This rear wing is showing serious rust. It is repairable but at a cost.

Replacement of rear wheelarches is possible, but does involve welding and respraying, making it a fairly costly job. It is much simpler to avoid a car needing rear wings, especially as this is so easy to spot.

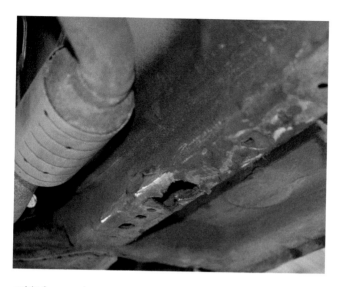

A quick look underneath this example reveals a large rust hole. Unless you want to be involved in an in-depth welding repair, this car would probably best be avoided.

guide for panel gaps on most cars is to think of a £1 or 1€ coin. Would the coin run all the way around a panel gap without getting stuck. If the gap gets narrower or wider there is an issue. Badly fitting panels rust! Does it have a tatty hood, or kerbed wheels? How do the tyres look? Is the windscreen cracked? How are the headlights? Cloudy or clear? All these points can be noticed as you walk up to and past the car on the owner's driveway. Don't be afraid to walk away at this point. A polite "I'm sorry, it's not really what I am looking for," is all you need. If all is good however, knock on the door and start the once over!

Shiny black undersides can mean a well-loved and protected car ... or a recent coat of cheap underseal to cover up rot. If the coating looks this fresh you should ask to see a receipt from a reputable repairer or chassis protection specialist, otherwise treat with extreme caution.

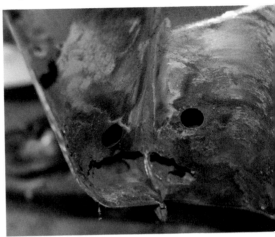

Investigate behind the felt rear wheelarch liner. As you can see, access is tight …

… but neglecting to check could leave you open to finding this later. Rot has taken hold.

Exterior

As stated above, you are looking for an exterior that is straight and clean. These cars were built by robots, so panel gaps should be perfect; the coin test mentioned above is a useful guide and can be used on most cars. It's not a problem if there is a difference in gaps, so long as they are even. For instance, the door should have an equal gap all the way round, and it should be similar to the bonnet and the bootlid. What you do not want to see is a gap that starts wide at one end tapering to nothing at the other.

Now let's look for rust. This is the big one. You need a torch and those magic thumbs. On hands and knees, firstly look along the bottom of the side skirts; it's not uncommon to see surface rust along the sill flange here. If the sill is body coloured (not black unless the car is) then that's a good sign. If it is black, this suggests it has been painted over, as the sill lips would originally have been body colour – that isn't necessarily an issue, so long as it's consistent with a caring owner, and not a cover up. What you don't want to see is rot. If this area is rotten it bodes badly for the rest of the car.

The number one rust spot for Mk3s is behind the felt arch liners in the rear wheelarches. It would be fantastic if a seller allowed you to remove them, but in the real world no one would permit this. You can check this area by lifting up the bottom of the liner. You will see one of two things before lifting: either an 8mm headed bolt/screw with a washer under it, or a hole in the felt and no screw. What commonly happens is this area rots and gets repaired, but the screw isn't replaced. This isn't a huge issue; what matters is that the repair has been done well. So lift the flap, screw or no screw, and have a look. If it's rotten with holes

The aluminium bootlid can suffer surface corrosion – unsightly, even if not structural.

through here, it isn't a deal breaker provided you don't mind a project, and may be cheaper to resolve than you think. But it is a hassle you may not want. Do not assume anything: the author has seen early cars with no rot here and late cars on which the arch fell away with the liner. Check every one. If the screw is present and the liner pulls off easily, it is simple to wriggle it back into position once you have finished checking.

The inner wheelarches were often very poorly painted or protected, the studs with the plastic nuts seem to have had no paint at all, and it's common to find them rusted away entirely. The felt liner is almost perfectly designed to hold water and salt against this metalwork, with the effect that everywhere it touches rots through. This can be fairly serious around the studs with the plastic nuts, but can also lead to fist-sized holes around the lower screw, which may just pull out with its grommet from the rusty bodywork. Water can then collect on a shelf inside (the floor of the sill) and rot through the vertical diaphragm that forms part of the sill structure. The first time this issue is usually noticed is when the car fails its MOT because of a hole in the bottom of the sill. Welding does not cure the cause of the problem, which is the water coming in from above. Seeing a properly executed repair in this corner area of the arch is fine, but if this problem is allowed to go unchecked, the repair becomes more complicated and expensive.

The next area to check is under the rear bumper. Rust in this area is common, although rarely serious. Look as best as you can up past the exhaust to see what you can see. It's unlikely you will see much even if you have it on a ramp, and in most cases this area gets a bit of surface rust and no more.

Front wings can rot, but this is quite easy to spot; they tend to rust around the wheelarch, and especially around the indicator hole.

The underbody can be fairly horrible-looking on these cars without being inherently bad; I am always wary of a car that has a fresh coating of underseal, especially if it is the cheap spray-on type beloved by bodgers, as it is often hiding rot. The underbody should show very little sign of rust, but if it does make a note for your more detailed check later. Rusty suspension components and underbody bracing aren't much to worry about. The floor along the sills is very rarely rusty, but, if it is, this suggests the shell has had serious water ingress issues and the car is best avoided.

Bonnets can develop unsightly corrosion around stone chips; this won't get much worse as it's aluminium, but it can ruin the look of an otherwise tidy car, so it's worth catching early. Soft tops have alloy bootlids which can corrode on the underside; PRHT models have steel bootlids, so tend to be worse affected if rust sets in.

Engine bay and running
Make sure the engine isn't running when you arrive: ideally, you want to check the engine cold first. Don't be afraid to stop the seller from starting the engine.

This engine bay is filthy but sound, and will clean up like new with a bit of work.
Have a thorough look around.

Check that oil level!

Lift the bonnet and prop it open. If it's windy, ask your companion or the seller to hold it, to prevent a potential accident.

Firstly, look around, how does it look? Mk3s tend to have very clean engine bays, even on tatty-looking, high-mileage cars. Don't worry about dust and grime, but you do not want to be seeing rot, particularly around the top of the wheelarches where the arch liners fasten with plastic rivets, or signs of leaking fluids anywhere (it isn't uncommon to see a bit of moisture around the power steering upper pipes and reservoir, but they should never be actively leaking).

Feel the top of the engine – is it cold? If not, it's possible the seller has just been for a drive, or they could have been warming it up to hide a cold start issue, though this is less of a problem on a Mk3 than some other cars.

Next, remove the dipstick, wipe and replace, then check the oil level, assuming the car is on the flat. Is it close to the maximum? How dirty is the oil? How does it smell? A well looked after Mk3 will have the oil maintained close to maximum. If the oil is nice and clean that's great, so long as the car has been recently serviced, but if it hasn't, it could be burning so much oil it never gets a chance to get dirty – laughable but true!

Check the other fluids: water, brake and clutch fluid, and power steering fluid. They should look nice and fresh, but also do a general check for suitable levels. If they are worryingly low, it may be worth walking away from. Look at the auxiliary belt (what would have been called the fanbelt): does it look old?

You can now have the engine started: watch the rear of the car for exhaust smoke (rare in a Mk3 as it generally gets caught by the catalytic converter), then listen to the engine for any unusual sounds, especially a knocking noise. If you

A small cubby hole off to the side of the boot holds the jack and tool kit.

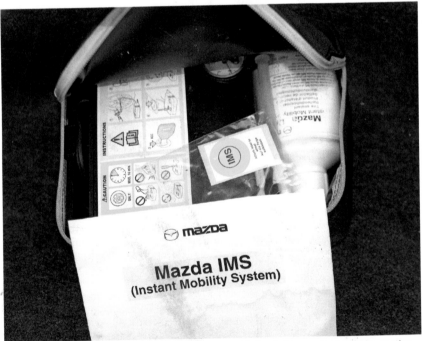

The Mazda Instant Mobility System is a repair kit for flat tyres. It should be on the back wall of the boot.

hear a tiny rattle for half a second or so on initial start-up of a cold engine that is completely normal, but be very wary if you hear a deep knock, especially on revving the engine to 1-2k rpm. This knock may go away at higher revs or become even louder, but it is generally noticeable when revving at this level. This noise is not hydraulic tappets, a loose timing chain, or any other potentially cheap faults that the seller might claim it to be, it is most likely to be the big end bearing on number one conrod that has failed due to a low oil event.

In rare cases the noise could indicate a failing idler or tensioner on the auxiliary belt. The only reliable way to test this is to remove the belt and start the engine: if the noise goes away, great! Now the belt just needs refitting – a much nicer job than replacing the engine, but not many sellers would be willing to do this for you. In the author's experience, nine out of ten times the cause of the knocking is the big end bearings that have gone.

Interior and boot
Now, pop open the boot. There is no spare wheel in a MK3, but there is a puncture repair kit usually strapped to the back wall of the boot, as well as a jack and tool roll which are in the right hand cubby at the side (as you look in to the boot). Boot leaks are not unknown on Mk3s, is it damp, mouldy or smelly? Lift the carpet, any rust?

Finally move on to the inside of the car. Check and operate all of the electrical

Check the condition of the interior, and make sure everything works.

components: lights, windscreen wipers, electric windows, stereo, air-con (if fitted), fan, dash lights, heated seats (if fitted), electric mirrors, etc – if there is a button, test it. There isn't much in a Mk3, so it doesn't take long, and the electrics are usually very reliable. One thing to note about electric windows: on Mk1 and 2 MX-5s it is common for the electric windows to be slow, this is not the case on a Mk3, so if the windows are slow something is wrong.

As you can see, this interior has been modified substantially, and the owner has intentionally removed many original features. If buying a car like this, ask the seller if they still have the original parts – if you wanted to return the car to standard it could save you a lot of money.

8 Key points
– where to look for problems

Body

Look closely and feel around all four wheelarches for corrosion (be careful of sharp edges). Be realistic: if the car is priced high and described as perfect, you should expect perfection, but if it is cheap and described as usable, expect some corrosion on the back edge of the arches. Also check for poor quality repairs involving filler.

Check around the front wing side repeaters, this is a classic Mk3 rust spot.

Check around the top of the sill covers where they meet the rear wings, this is a common area for rear wings to start showing rust. If present, it is probably creeping up from below, and will be much more serious where you can't see it.

Inside the rear wheelarches you will find a liner made of carpet-like material: lift this up at the bottom and have a good press and poke – if you feel any softness or see holes, this area will need repair.

The front wing side repeater holes are well known for rusting, so check them carefully. A new wing is the fix at this stage.

Interior

While generally hard wearing, sometimes you will encounter missing or broken trim, or torn seats. Leather seats tend to wear better than cloth, but it is not unusual for wear on the driver's side bolsters of either type. You may also find that owners have modified their cars, and can be a matter of personal taste.

Electrics

Generally, Mk3 electrics are extremely reliable; however, dashboard warning lights are relatively common. Seeing an engine warning light is not too much of a concern but the issue will need investigating, if the seller hasn't already done this. The most common cause is a faulty lambda/oxygen sensor in the exhaust system. ABS warning lights are also common. Diagnostic work will usually need to be carried out at a garage where the car can be plugged into a computer, via the onboard diagnostics port. Radios can suffer poor reception if a stubby aerial is fitted, and where Bose stereos are fitted, check the speakers for crackling or popping.

This interior shows a badly worn driver's seat, as well as a non-standard gearknob and gaiter.

The Bose stereo (fitted to an NC1 here) can have some reliability issues. The system can be replaced with more modern components, which is often cheaper than a repair.

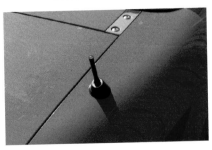

A stubby aerial may look better (personal taste) but the reception is usually much poorer.

Engine

Listen to the engine, can you hear tapping, knocking or rattling at any revs? If so, it could potentially be the serious big end knock that affects this model if the oil has been allowed to drop low. It is highly unlikely to be a rattling pulley or tappet as some sellers claim.

Gearbox

All gearboxes, including the automatic, are utterly reliable, provided service schedules are followed. The five-speed manual tends to be a robust and faultless unit, with a lovely shift; the six-speed manual is also tough and reliable, but can suffer a notchy shift, usually due to not having had the oil changed in the gearbox, or the wrong oil being used. There is also a shift plate on top of the gearbox which sometimes causes this problem in first and second gear, but this can be changed at very minimal cost. Rare, but notchy shifting while stationary, which goes away once moving, is a sign of a failing clutch hydraulic system.

Listen carefully to the engine: rev it slightly (to around 2500rpm) and listen on the way up and down for a noise like a heavy chain being rattled. Ignore the partially lifted dipstick shown in this picture – it's not part of the procedure.

The automatic should shift smoothly from cold, with no excess slipping or shuddering. If either are experienced, exercise caution, as it is likely to be an expensive repair. If the seller claims it just needs a fluid change to resolve they should be willing to get that done before purchase, as it is a minimal cost; if they are reluctant to do this you should consider why.

Big end knock concerns the piston and conrod, as seen here. The bearing at the big end of the conrod may be damaged, allowing it to rattle on the crankshaft.

9 Serious evaluation

– 60 minutes for years of enjoyment

Score each section using the boxes as follows:
4 = Excellent; 3 = good; 2 = average; 1 = poor. The totting up procedure is detailed at the end of the chapter. Be realistic in your marking.

Use the tools you brought with you, as detailed in chapter 6. Now you will be looking over the following items very closely indeed, and by the end of this check you will potentially know the car better than the owner. A helpful technique as you wander round the car and notice issues, is to touch them with your hand, it doesn't need to be an over-the-top gesture, just a brief touch – the owner will realise you have spotted an issue and will be adding up all these negatives in their head just as you are. When the time comes to negotiate, they will have already started to talk themselves down, and it quite often saves the awkward and confrontational approach of having to list all the faults as justification of a lower price. Of course you should be fair, especially if the seller has been open about faults, and listed the car at a price that takes them in to account.

Paperwork
This section is not scored, purely as we all place different value on paperwork and the supporting items. Personally, I like a car to have both keys, its original 'book pack' or the handbook and pouch it came with, and a history folder, along with its legal documents. I have to admit though, that I have bought terrible cars with all those in place, and great cars with them missing. However, as a minimum, you should always have the registration document or title for the car, and a roadworthiness certificate (an MOT in the UK – these are now issued as digital certificates, so you may want to see proof online if a paper copy is not available). Some history and service records are also good to see, unless there is a valid reason for them to be missing and the car is priced accordingly. Missing paperwork will devalue any car, making it harder to sell in the future.

Always check through the paperwork carefully, and make sure names and registration numbers match.

A first look at this car shows a very good-looking example of an early Mk3; however, closer inspection reveals rust around the wheelarches. Although repairable, this will incur a substantial cost for welding and painting.

Exterior of car

Consider the exterior of the car as a whole. Hopefully it will be clean, which will make the job much easier. If it is dirty or covered in moss, it is advisable to wipe off the surface with a cloth in all the common rot spots, so you can see issues. How is the paintwork? If the paint is beyond rescue a full respray is not cheap. When checking the condition of the bodywork and panels, keep in mind the difference in repair costs between panels; changing a fuel flap is much cheaper and easier than changing a back wing, while front wings, doors, or bumpers are also easier to replace as they unbolt.

Paintwork

Resolving minor paint issues need not be hugely expensive, but if the car needs a full respray that might easily exceed the value of the car. Thankfully, Mk3 paintwork is resilient, so you should only see wear in the form of damage, if you see faded paint or lacquer peel, or especially bad paint reactions, this suggests previous paintwork has been done poorly. Look over each panel carefully.

Checking paint is much easier if the car is clean; sellers know this, so always be a bit suspicious if the car is absolutely filthy. Be prepared to wipe away dirt in certain areas so you can check the paintwork thoroughly.

Stand back from the car and really look at the paint, look for different colour shades and finishes. A factory paint finish on one of these cars has the same finish across the entire car, and colour match across the car should be perfect. If the bumpers are a slightly different shade, don't believe the seller who says it's because

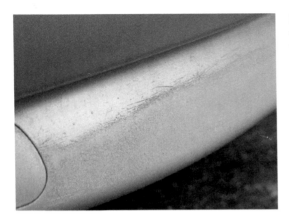

Not all paint defects are this obvious, and this certainly won't polish out.

they are plastic. While this does affect some cars it is not a shortcoming of the Mk3 MX-5, the colour match is excellent as standard, the actual paint finish should be too. There is barely any orange peel found on these cars. If you can find a reflection of something like a nearby post mirrored on the bodywork, you will get a good impression of the finish very easily.

Check paintwork in these areas:
• Front bumper – look for stone chips and scratches, especially underneath where it might have been bashed into kerbs.
• Bonnet – look for stone chips, and the tell-tale worm tracks of water creeping under the paint due to the aluminium corroding.
• Sills – look for scuffs and scratches, check around the jacking points, has a jack been rammed into the skirt?
• Front wings – Due to the wide protruding wings on the Mk3 they can sometimes be caught on gate posts and the like, so check for damage – not just rust, but dents, scratches and scuffs, and also evidence of poor quality paint repairs. DIY repairs using an aerosol can are unlikely to last long.
• Doors – look for scuffs and scratches.

Left: When a stone chip damages the paint on an alloy panel, you get blisters and worm tracks under the paint. These are unsightly, but won't rust through.
Right: The front bumper is particularly vulnerable to stone chips.

• Rear wings – look around the wheelarches, the rear arches also protrude from the shell. Check the areas where the sills, rear bumper and rear lights meet the panel. Are there signs of rubbing or scuffs?

• Rear bumper – check for scuffs and scratches.

• Infill panel between rear wings – there is only likely to be damage here if a hardtop has been fitted clumsily, but check it anyway.

• Windscreen surround – this area is vulnerable to stone chips and even corrosion, especially if the windscreen has been refitted carelessly. Have a close look; repainting this panel is a time-consuming and costly job.

Body panels

Now it's time to get up close and personal with the panels on the car. You have looked at the paintwork, now you are looking for damage, rust, dents, etc … basically anything that compromises the structure of the bodywork. As well as the obvious problems, you should also keep a look out for poor repairs. Can you see filler or scratches from rubbing down around the panel? Here, you will consider each panel type individually, and score accordingly.

Bumpers   [4] [3] [2] [1]

Look for dents in the plastic from possible rubbing against posts or other minor accident damage. Check the main face for parking damage, and also check for cracks all over the panel. Where you do see damage, is it fresh (ie, it's happened and been left), or has it had an attempted repair, such as filler, paint etc? If the damage is near another panel edge look at that, too, as it may also have been damaged and repaired or replaced. Build up a complete picture. Are the bumpers secure? Grab the edges and give them a gentle wiggle, they shouldn't flap around.

Front wings   [4] [3] [2] [1]

Dents and rust are the main issues here: look for dents on the wheelarch edges, or rust on wheelarch edges and around the indicator. Rectification isn't very expensive or difficult, but you'll want the car to be priced accordingly. There should be a VIN sticker attached to the inside of the wings, which is visible when the bonnet is lifted, and this should match the car's VIN. If missing or different, this suggests the car has had new paintwork or a replacement panel.

Check the front wings for rust and look at the flange where the bonnet rests. A chassis number sticker should be present.

Sill covers

Check along the sill covers for damage such as scuffs or cracks where the jacking points have been missed, or the car has clouted something down low. Also check for looseness, it might point to the cover having been removed – not a big deal, but again can be an indicator of other issues.

Look carefully at the sill covers; they are robust but can be damaged.

Rear wings

Check again for rust: around the arch lip, where it meets the sill cover, check panel gaps with sill covers and rear bumper AND the bootlid. The most likely part to be misaligned is the rear bumper; if it is, has the bumper been rubbing the paint away on the wing and allowed rust to take hold?

Check the rear wing all over, but especially the arch lip. This arch is starting to rust.

Doors

You may find small parking dents, but the door panels are curved and strong, as well as being reasonably thick metal, so they aren't prone to dents. Rust would be unusual, and a big red flag for past damage and poor repairs. Run your fingers carefully around the opened door edge, roughness should be checked by eye, it may have

A small ding in the door isn't unusual. A dent specialist could get this out.

Again, a chassis number sticker is present. This is the original door.

been caused by a chip or rust. There should also be a VIN sticker attached to the inside rearmost edge of the door, this should match the car's VIN. If missing or different it points to new paintwork or a replacement panel.

Bonnet

The bonnet is likely to have some stone chips, but it should not have dents. Check the stone chips carefully, have they been touched in? If not, has corrosion started? It's an aluminium bonnet, so is not going to rust through, but it will become unsightly as more paint flakes off. Lift the bonnet, is the liner in place and in good condition? Corrosion is unusual inside the bonnet. You should see another VIN sticker on the underside of the bonnet lid.

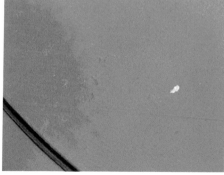

Stone chips and aluminium corrosion can be unsightly.

The chassis number sticker is present, and this is the original bonnet.

Bootlid and infill panel between rear wings

The painted face of the bootlid should be perfect. Check the rear edge where it drops to meet the bumper: damage here raises suspicion of a rear end impact. Check panel gaps around the boot; again, these should all be equal, if not it suggests the bootlid has been removed at the very least. There should be another VIN sticker attached to the inside, visible when the bootlid is lifted, which should again match the car's VIN. On soft tops it is common (although not good) for the area where the number plate lights are fitted to have flaking paint due to alloy corrosion. It isn't the biggest job to sort out, and the metal is almost always perfectly solid, but it can be very unsightly. The infill panel should exhibit no structural damage or rust.

Alloy corrosion can be repainted; at least the panel isn't rotten.

Windscreen surround

The main thing to check here is rust. If windscreens are fitted without care then the paint can be damaged, allowing water to rust the metal, and before long it creeps into the windscreen frame. Repairs to this area are expensive, and usually involve

Check the windscreen frame – it's rarely rusty, but hugely expensive to repair if it is.

removing and replacing the windscreen. The author's usual advice would be to steer clear unless the car is very cheap.

Exterior trim

This includes anything that isn't a body panel – all the odd bits that make up the rest of the outside of the car. Plastic parts in particular need attention; where they are damaged they are usually easy to replace, but costs do add up. Black parts that have faded can be brought back to look like new using various trim restorers, but the faded look can be a good bargaining point.

Mirrors, door handles, quarter light frames

The mirrors on these cars are relatively fragile when struck, look for deep gouges or cracks in the body, check the glass for cracks.

The door handles are strong and rarely damaged, just check they work and make sure the key works in the lock.

The quarter light frames between the main window and the small quarter light window are prone to rusting. They can be rubbed down and painted or replaced,

Rust on the quarterlight frames is common. This could be a good bargaining point, as it's time-consuming to fix.

This car has had a scrape on the bumper. Although the damage isn't serious, it still needs to be repaired, and could be missed if the car is dirty.

but the door will need to be stripped down, so if there is rust here the price of the car should take this into account.

Bumper grilles, towing eye covers, number plates, badges
Check the bumper grilles, towing eye covers and number plates for cracks or damage (or note if they are missing). It may be a small job to resolve, but costs add up. Make sure the badges are present and undamaged, it is not unknown for owners to debadge cars, or modify the front Mazda logo by cutting it so it looks like it has devil horns. Also check the badges haven't been painted, if they have been rubbed down to be painted (usually black) then just removing the paint won't help, and they ought to be replaced.

The small bits of trim like towing eye covers are rarely missing on Mk3s, but always be aware how expensive these can be.

Windscreen scuttle/wipers, chrome hardtop mounts, radio aerial
Check the windscreen scuttle, especially the two small oval covers that cover the mounting screws at the outside edges. They are often missing, though the cost is minimal. Also look over the wipers, make sure the blades are in decent condition and the arms aren't rusty.
There are two chrome hardtop mounting plates that go between the rear wings

The wiper blades often suffer from paint loss, but is easy to resolve with satin black paint.

and the infill panel between the wings. Check the condition, they are plastic, so won't be rusty. Check the screws: if all four screws are the same, the car does not have the hardtop mounting package fitted, but if it has two normal screws and a pair of bobbin shaped screws that stick up, these are to mount the hardtop on.

The radio aerials on these cars often deteriorate. Take a look, and also see if it unscrews – the genuine aerials rarely seize in, but if an aftermarket aerial has been fitted they frequently do.

Hood or roof

On PRHT cars check the condition of the roof (don't worry yet about operating the roof). PRHT roofs frequently fade badly, as do the lift up covers that move to allow the

The fantastic PRHT roof in operation. Make sure it works: while usually reliable it would be expensive to repair.

This soft top is tired. It can be treated and improved with a renovation product, but replacement is the only way to make it perfect again.

roof to fold in to the storage cavity. It may already have been repainted, perhaps in black, or been vinyl wrapped – both look nice but neither are cheap.

Soft top roofs should be in good condition, they are not prone to wear or damage like earlier models, and they are very cheap secondhand because of this, but it could be a good bargaining point if a car has a torn roof.

Roofs often get damaged by mosses and lichens growing in the fabric. This can usually be cleaned up, however.

Finally, if a hardtop is fitted, check its condition, but also make sure you get it removed to check the soft top. Although the Mk3 roof is very tough and rarely damaged, never assume anything – the fabric could be split or have been vandalised, and you can't be sure unless you see it in place.

Glass

Don't expect huge issues here, but a check is advisable. Look over each piece of glass in detail, check the windscreen for chips, scratches or cracks, and check around the edges for delamination. Damage will generally only be resolved with a new screen, so it's worth the look. Check the side windows and the rear window,

Glass and lights should all be checked. This headlight is fogged, but the lens can be polished.

both inside and out. It is common for both the driver's and passenger's windows to get vertical scratches on the outside from grit trapped in the seal, as well as random scratches inside from ring wearers.

Underside

It will be a major advantage if you are able to get under the car, using a ramp if you are at a garage, or if the owner is willing for you to turn up with a trolley jack and axle stands. However, NEVER EVER go under a car that is supported only on a jack. And only consider jacking up the car and using stands if you are experienced and confident you can do so safely.

Consider the underside as a whole. Include checks into the rear wheelarches

The underside of Mk3s is rarely pretty, but the main problem you are looking for is rusty suspension. (There are missing bolts in this example due to ongoing work.)

Work on the suspension can involve a heavy impact gun to break free rusty bolts.

The floor rarely has much rust ...

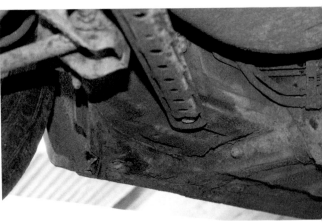

... except here, where the rear wheelarch has rotted through to the underside.

especially, go as far as the owner will permit, get the wheels off if you can, and the arch liner out. It would be a rare Mk3 with no corrosion here, and an even rarer owner who wasn't shocked. Better the current owner be shocked than you.

Follow the rear arch down to where it meets the sill and floor area, poke this area as well as you can, a strong thumb is enough to flex rusty metal, or, if the owner allows, a gentle nudge with a tool can be useful. Take care not to scratch the paint or underseal if present: scratching rust is one thing, scratching a protected surface is not acceptable, as you will create a future rust issue. Look along the bottom of the sills: some surface rust is common, but bubbles, while rarely serious on these cars, will need attention sooner rather than later. Have a good look at the rear bulkhead underneath (the bit your bottom sits against); it's rare but rust can hide here. Also look around the rear subframe up into the shell if the opportunity presents; a powerful torch will be useful.

Check under the rear bumper between the exhaust box and bumper: some light surface rust is common, but occasionally the crash bar is completely rotten. Provided it hasn't spread to the body this is fairly easy to rectify, as it's a bolt-off item, and fairly cheap.

Look over suspension arms, brakes, brake pipes (especially the flexible rubber pipes to the calipers). Again, some rust is completely normal, but are they rotten? With regard to suspension arms, look at the bushes and ball joints: the rubber bushes and the rubber ball joint covers will give you a good feel for the condition of the arm itself. On a cheaper Mk3 replacing worn suspension arms could easily exceed a third of the value of the car, not including labour. Add the cost of new brakes and a bit of rust repair, and you realise why these checks are needed.

The exhaust should also be inspected, mainly the mid-pipe where it meets the back box. It is common for this area to rot. You won't generally hear it from outside, but once serious rot sets in it is only a matter of time before the mid-pipe separates

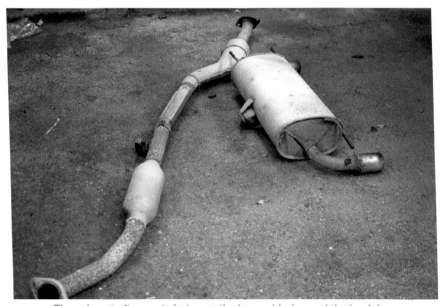

The exhaust often rusts between the long mid-pipe and the back box.

from the box. Thankfully, if this happens it doesn't usually drop down, but it is a hassle you do not want. Stainless replacements are cheap and easy to fit, as are repair sections.

The final thing to check (if you can) is the clutch slave cylinder. This is mounted on the opposite side of the gearbox to the exhaust. It is usually hard to see due to underbody covers, but if it is visible check it isn't damp. The Mk3 clutch slave is very reliable, unlike earlier cars, and replacement is cheap and easy.

Car mechanicals

Now you have finished with the exterior of the car, move on to the actual mechanics of the vehicle. There will be a limit as to what you can check, but the following should help provide a practical and pragmatic approach to checking over the mechanics, as well as satisfying yourself it is a car you are willing to take for a test drive.

This exhaust is in good condition, but this is the area most likely to fail.

4   3   2   1

Wheels, tyres and brakes

These have been grouped together, as checking them should be done at the same time.

Look over the wheels, checking for scratches, chips, kerbing damage, etc. If you can get under the car, spin the wheels to look for flat spots on the tyres: the Mk3 has quite soft wheels, so flat spots are not unusual. Are locking wheel nuts fitted? If so, look for the key later. If the wheels have been removed by you and you need to reattach, the wheel nut torque is around 103Nm or 76ftlb. In the owner's handbook Mazda claims a fairly wide range, however, of 88-118Nm or 65-87ftlb. Going in the middle will give you a margin of error on most torque wrenches.

Tyres should be checked for tread depth. A British 20p coin slipped into the grooves in the tread can make an excellent tread depth tester: if the raised edge of the coin is obscured by tread the tyre is good, but if visible the tyre may be illegal. Tyre laws vary by country, but in the UK the legal minimum tread is 1.6mm ($\frac{1}{16}$ in) across the centre 75% of the tyre tread. What is not legal in any country are damaged or bald tyres, or those exhibiting any of the following – chunks of tread missing, wires/bands showing through, bulges (delamination with a blown up section on the sidewall from damage), or bad cracking. Check that the tyres are the correct size – either 205/50 R16 or 205/45 R17 on most models. If the opportunity to check pressure exists, this should be 29psi or 2.0 bar. Tyres must be the same size across an axle, and the same brand, model and age across an axle. Take note of the tyre brand. A new set of budget tyres may be a selling point, but make

Use a torch to inspect general brake condition.

ownership miserable, these cars are sensitive to tyre choice and suspension set up – cheap nasty tyres will affect handling and, most importantly, grip. On the other hand, a newish set of premium tyres can be a good indication of a well looked after car.

Finally, look for the date code on the tyres, this will be a four digit code in an oval window on the tyre sidewall, usually close to the wheel rim, an example of this code would be 0512 or 0920, the first two numbers are the week the tyre was made, the last two are the year. So in our example, the first tyre was made in week five of 2012, a very old tyre now, the second was made in week nine of 2020.

A coin can be used to check tyre tread depth.

Tyres over five years old really need replacing, regardless of tread depth; rubber deteriorates with age and old tyres can blow out, especially if the car has been sitting for long periods without moving. A set of new tyres is a small price to pay for peace of mind.

Finally look at the brakes, you can see a lot through the wheel. Look at the disc, the swept surface back and front if you can. Is there pitting or score marks? If so, the discs will need replacing. If the disc is smooth, feel with a finger the swept surface to the outer edge (before doing this make sure the car has not just been driven or they will be very hot and burn you!). Is there a large step up? This shows how much wear that disc has, and if substantial it may also need replacing. Now look at the pads. You will only be able to see the outers, and requires careful positioning of a torch and your eye, but try to gauge how much pad is left. Less than 1mm is danger territory, and they need replacing asap, especially as you are only checking half the pads in the car and they rarely wear totally evenly.

Now take a quick visual look at the calipers. Do they look new or old? Nothing wrong with older calipers, but, if they look very rusty and tired, chances are they may need some work soon. A quick check of the handbrake can be done by pulling it on, making sure the car doesn't roll, then taking it off and ensuring the car rolls without catching. The Mk3 rear calipers are reliable, but this test catches out a lot of cars, especially with the roll after release, as the calipers get sticky with age.

Suspension

The checks you are able to do for the suspension are very limited, and you learn much more on the test drive, but a very quick bounce test on each corner will

expose a completely failed shock absorber. As a guide, the car shouldn't really move much as you press down and should come straight back up and stop. If it bounces up and down some work is needed.

Engine bay

The following checks of the mechanicals are by far the most important, and where you should spend most of your time.

Using your torch, and with the engine off, have a good look around the engine bay. Look for rust on the shell (although this is a bodywork issue, check while you are here). Next, turn your torch to the exhaust system you can see in the engine

Mk3 shock absorbers are fairly reliable, but a visual inspection and bounce test may reveal a failing shock.

A look around the engine bay may reveal interesting modifications, such as this exhaust manifold ...

... or perhaps a generally well cared for engine bay that is tidy, albeit not especially clean.

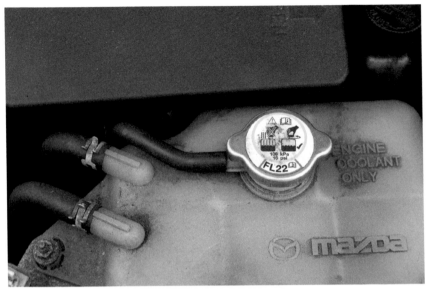

Check the coolant; it should be clean and green.
As the cap says, FL22 coolant only.

bay, it should look perfect, as they are not prone to rust here. Check for leaks around the steering rack and power steering pump and reservoir. Look down the side of the engine for leaks, too. If you find any, track them back to where they came from. If there is an oil stain on the engine, follow its trail upwards to see where it came from: if it carries on to the top it may have overflowed when being clumsily filled, or it could be a leaking cam cover seal. Check the coolant hoses, do they look in decent condition? Look at the aux belt: is it cracked where it bends over the pulleys? If so the belt needs changing soon. Look at the radiator: can you see brown staining on the front or rear face, or obvious dampness? This could indicate a leak. Check the coolant: is the coolant fresh looking (usually green special FL22 coolant), or is it murky and dirty? Worse still, is it clear water? If so, walk away – that car is likely to be dropping or using coolant, and has been topped up with water to the point it's now clear.

Check the oil level: if the original cup type dipstick is fitted (early cars) they are easier to read from the back. The later dipsticks were improved. Look at the brake fluid (shared with the clutch): is it a clean golden fluid or murky brown? Dip the power steering tank, check it just like you do the engine oil: pull the dipstick out at the top, wipe on a clean rag, replace dipstick, remove and check level.

You can't check the gearbox or diff oil on these cars without a good deal of effort, so you will need to listen for unusual drivetrain noise when on the test drive.

Take a general look over the engine bay: what is the overall impression? Is it clean and cared for, or tired and dirty? Does it match the rest of the car? You should also keep in mind the things you noticed during your 15 minute check, such as engine running, knocking noises, or smoke from the exhaust.

The original hard to read dipstick at the top, and the improved version below.

Interior and electrics

In this section you will check everything else. I usually like to ask the seller at this point if it is okay to go into the boot and other areas on the car. People keep all sorts in their cars, so it's only polite to ask, and it might save you a nasty surprise too!

Boot   4 3 2 1

The boot can be considered as one area. Inside you should see plastic panels all the way round the sides, and a carpeted floor. On the back wall there should be a puncture repair kit containing some basic tools for the job, a compressor, and a can of repair sealant. If the sealant is not there you need to know where it is – it could be inside the car for instance – but if missing it should be replaced, as the car has no spare wheel. Off to the right side of the boot is a cubby hole with a flap, inside which should be a jack and toolkit containing a towing eye, wheel brace, and jack handle. PRHT cars will also have some string, an Allen key and a threaded rod to assist in raising the roof if the mechanism fails.

Seats   4 3 2 1

Move the seats in all positions; check the condition of the fabric or leather coverings, including the rear of the seats. Can you see tears, scuffs, or collapsed foam?

Door cards   4 3 2 1

What is the overall condition? Are there any missing parts? Is the door card secure in the door or have the clips broken?

Carpet   4 3 2 1

Check the general condition. Are there cigarette burns? Is it dirty or stained? Is there wear from driver's heels under the pedals?

Interior plastic trim   4 3 2 1

Examine all the plastic trim, operate the flaps on the cubby holes behind the seats, the cubby on rear of centre console, the cup holder on the centre console, and the glovebox. Check none of the trim is missing or cracked.

Check the seats for rips and tears. Here, a slight scuff on the bolster can be recoloured easily.

Check the door cards; higher spec models have leather inserts, as here.

A small tear but costly to put right. Replacing the carpet is a very involved job.

The plastic panel behind the seats is a large piece with integrated lids: check the condition, latches, etc.

Steering wheel, gearknob and pedals

Check the general condition: look for tears or wear on the steering wheel or gearknob cover, or a missing pedal cover. These parts don't wear fast, so can be a useful indication of genuine mileage. If they look utterly destroyed on a low mileage car, it has had an interesting past.

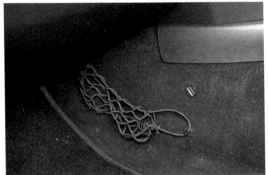

Check the net in the passenger footwell – it often breaks (as here).

Gearknobs are vulnerable to ring-wearers, and may get scratched. Likewise the steering wheel.

The fuel lid release is in the cubby hole between the seats (left). The bonnet and boot release are in the driver's footwell (right).

Check that the stereo and cd player work.

Electrics and operation

[4] [3] [2] [1]

Operate everything. Every light, wiper, heated rear screen, air-con, hazards, horn, washer, electric mirrors and windows. Operate the roof on soft top and PRHT cars. Make sure the radio works. If there is a CD changer (Bose multichanger head unit) insert more than one CD to make sure it works. Check that the steering wheel controls for the radio work. Check that the central locking works; check the boot release with the button next to the bonnet release (check that, too), as well as the one on the key.

Check the dash warning lights, both now and during the test drive. Needless to say, none should be illuminated.

The test drive

[4] [3] [2] [1]

This section is scored as one item. The last thing you want on a test drive is to be mentally taking score. Judge it when you return.

This is what all the checks have been leading up to: you are happy with the car, and you want to move on to the final step – the drive – before negotiations. You have ensured the car is legally roadworthy, in terms of both paperwork and having checked the safety of the vehicle (your inspection has also been an excellent safety check!). You are legally able to drive the car, holding the correct licence and insurance, and are not under the influence of anything that means you shouldn't drive.

The purpose of the test drive is to ensure that not only is the car in good working order, but also that it is the car you want. Test drives usually take about

15 minutes or so; not too long. You don't want to come back crippled because of the seat position, so firstly try to adjust the seat so that you are comfortable. If it can't be overcome, walk away. If you hated driving the car for 15 minutes you are unlikely to love driving it home, or want to take it out after that. On the other hand, driving a car for the first time, with the owner sitting next to you, can be daunting, so it is normal to feel apprehensive. You would be an unusual person who could just jump into a new car and feel at home straight away, although if you can do that in any car it is this one.

It is usually best to let the owner drive the car on the outward journey: this serves two purposes, it lets you observe from the passenger seat, concentrate on noises, smoke from the back, seating positions, etc, and also gives you the opportunity to get an idea of how the owner drives. The wise seller will drive gently, but I have been out with sellers before who have redlined the car by the end of the street on a cold engine: this is an instant red flag for me and I will walk away from such a car – cold engines need to be warmed up properly, then they can be revved freely. The second advantage to the owner driving first is that it gets you off their drive, likely in an area you don't know. Most sellers will take you somewhere safe to swap over and get to know the car. I am reminded of the last car I bought where I was taken to a pub car park with very big speed bumps that the very low car barely went over, followed by a motorway in a few hundred yards. It was an interesting drive!

Take note of the following on your test drive:
• Engine – noises, smoke, smells. How does it pull? Does it seem flat? Is the temperature gauge too high/low? How does the exhaust sound? Is it quiet/noisy or is it blowing due to a hole? If you see smoke from the exhaust, white smoke or steam is water, and likely to be a head gasket issue, while blue or dirty smoke is likely to be oil. It would have to be burning a huge amount of oil for it to be visible in a Mk3. If the seller says they have never noticed it before, your reaction should be somewhere between sceptical and disbelieving.
• Gearbox – how does it change? All MX-5 manual boxes should feel nice to change; if it doesn't something is wrong; if it is crunching, something is very wrong.
• Clutch – is it slipping? Is it easy to depress?
• Brakes – do they feel right? They should feel solid and confidence-inspiring, no matter what you normally drive. There may be a touch more pedal travel than on some cars, but they should anchor up solidly. Find a deserted stretch of road and (making sure nothing is behind) brake hard – does the car pull to one side?
• Suspension and steering – does it feel direct and smooth? Can you hear knocks, creaks or rattles? Mk3s are prone to a rattle from the shocks. Not all suffer from it, and those that do are nothing to worry about, but many people find it annoying; new shocks will fix it.
• Drivetrain noise – by this time you should have a good feel for the car. Gently accelerate and decelerate: is there a whine which starts or stops as you change from accelerating to decelerating? If so it could be a worn diff. If there is a constant droning it is likely to be a wheel bearing.
• Comfort – get the roof down if you can for part of the drive (or up if it's down). What do you actually think of the car, are you loving it? You should! If the car has air-con, switch it on: it should go cold quickly now you are moving.

Let the engine idle for a couple of minutes, and see if the fan kicks in. Is there smoke from the back of the car? Switch off and wait five minutes, then check the oil: has it dropped? It shouldn't have. Do a visual check of the water level (DO NOT TAKE THE CAP OFF A HOT RADIATOR) – has it dropped?

Now is your chance to add up the scores and make your decision, but don't worry about mulling it over for half an hour. If you are sure, then strike while the iron is hot; the seller is in 'sell mode' – take advantage of it. But if you can't get close to a deal don't be afraid to walk; in a day or two the seller may be more amenable to a chat.

Evaluation procedure

Add up the total points score:

104 = perfect; 78 = good; 52 = average; 26 = poor.

Cars scoring over 73 should be completely usable and require the minimum of repair or rectification, although continued service maintenance and care will be required to keep them in good condition. Cars scoring between 26 and 53 will require serious work (at much the same cost regardless of score). Cars scoring between 54 and 72 will require very careful assessment of the necessary repair costs to decide whether to buy a better car for more money.

10 Auctions
– sold! Another way to buy your dream

Auction pros & cons

Pros: Prices will usually be lower than those of dealers or private sellers, and you might grab a real bargain on the day. Auctioneers have usually established clear title with the seller. At the venue you can usually examine documentation relating to the vehicle.

Cons: You have to rely on a sketchy catalogue description of condition and history. The opportunity to inspect is limited and you cannot drive the car. Auction cars are often a little below par and may require some work. It's easy to overbid. There will usually be a buyer's premium to pay in addition to the auction hammer price.

Which auction?

Auctions by established auctioneers are advertised in car magazines and on the auction houses' websites. A catalogue, or a simple printed list of the lots for auctions might only be available a day or two ahead, though often lots are listed and pictured on auctioneers' websites much earlier. Contact the auction company to ask if previous auction selling prices are available, as this is useful information (details of past sales are often available on websites).

It's easy to get carried away at car auctions, but look over the cars carefully and stick to your budget!

Catalogue, entry fee and payment details

When you purchase the catalogue of the vehicles in the auction, it often acts as a ticket allowing two people to attend the viewing days and the auction. Catalogue details tend to be comparatively brief, but will include information such as 'one owner from new, low mileage, full service history,' etc. It will also usually show a guide price to give you some idea of what to expect to pay and will tell you what is charged as a 'Buyer's premium.' The catalogue will also contain details of acceptable forms of payment. At the fall of the hammer an immediate deposit is usually required, the balance payable within 24 hours. If the plan is to pay by cash there may be a cash limit. Some auctions will accept payment by debit card. Sometimes credit or charge cards are acceptable, but will often incur an extra charge. A bank draft or bank transfer will have to be arranged in advance with your own bank as well as with the auction house. No car will be released before all payments are cleared. If delays occur in payment transfers then storage costs can accrue.

Buyer's premium

A buyer's premium will be added to the hammer price: don't forget this in your calculations. It is not usual for there to be a further state tax or local tax on the purchase price and/or on the buyer's premium.

Viewing

In some instances it's possible to view on the day, or days before, as well as in the hours prior to, the auction. There are auction officials available who are willing to help out by opening engine and luggage compartments and to allow you to inspect the interior. While the officials may start the engine for you, a test drive is out of the question. Crawling under and around the car as much as you want is permitted, but you can't suggest that the car you are interested in be jacked up, or attempt to do the job yourself. You can also ask to see any documentation available.

Bidding

Before you take part in the auction, decide your maximum bid – and stick to it!

It may take a while for the auctioneer to reach the lot you are interested in, so use that time to observe how other bidders behave. When it's the turn of your car, attract the auctioneer's attention and make an early bid. The auctioneer will then look to you for a reaction every time another bid is made, usually the bids will be in fixed increments until the bidding slows, when smaller increments will often be accepted before the hammer falls. If you want to withdraw from the bidding, make sure the auctioneer understands your intentions – a vigorous shake of the head when he or she looks to you for the next bid should do the trick!

Assuming that you are the successful bidder, the auctioneer will note your card or paddle number, and from that moment on you will be responsible for the vehicle.

If the car is unsold, either because it failed to reach the reserve or because there was little interest, it may be possible to negotiate with the owner, via the auctioneers, after the sale is over.

Successful bid

There are two more items to think about. How to get the car home, and insurance. If you can't drive the car, your own or a hired trailer is one way, another is to have the vehicle shipped using the facilities of a local company. The auction house will also have details of companies specialising in the transfer of cars.

Insurance for immediate cover can usually be purchased on site, but it may be more cost-effective to make arrangements with your own insurance company in advance, and then call to confirm the full details.

eBay & other online auctions?

eBay & other online auctions could land you a car at a bargain price, though you'd be foolhardy to bid without examining the car first, something most vendors encourage. A useful feature of eBay is that the geographical location of the car is shown, so you can narrow your choices to those within a realistic radius of home. Be prepared to be outbid in the last few moments of the auction. Remember, your bid is binding and that it will be very, very difficult to get restitution in the case of a crooked vendor fleecing you – caveat emptor!

Be aware that some cars offered for sale in online auctions are 'ghost' cars. Don't part with any cash without being sure that the vehicle does actually exist and is as described (usually pre-bidding inspection is possible).

Auctioneers

Barrett-Jackson: www.barrett-jackson.com
Bonhams: www.bonhams.com
British Car Auctions BCA: www.bca-europe.com or www.british-car-auctions.co.uk
Cheffins: www.cheffins.co.uk
Christies: www.christies.com
Coys: www.coys.co.uk
eBay: www.eBay.com
RM: www.rmauctions.com
Shannons: www.shannons.com.au
Silver: www.silverauctions.com

11 Paperwork
– correct documentation is essential!

The paper trail

At the time of writing the NC MX-5 may be a little too young for the following advice, but its time will come.

Classic, collector and prestige cars usually come with a large portfolio of paperwork accumulated and passed on by a succession of proud owners. This documentation represents the real history of the car, and from it can be deduced the level of care the car has received, how much it's been used, which specialists have worked on it and the dates of major repairs and restorations. All of this information will be priceless to you as the new owner, so be very wary of cars with little paperwork to support their claimed history.

Registration documents

All countries/states have some form of registration for private vehicles whether it's like the American 'pink slip' system or the British 'log book' system.

It is essential to check that the registration document is genuine, that it relates to the car in question, and that all the vehicle's details are correctly recorded, including chassis/VIN and engine numbers (if these are shown). If you are buying from the previous owner, his or her name and address will be recorded in the document: this will not be the case if you are buying from a dealer.

In the UK the current (Euro-aligned) registration document is named 'V5C,' and is printed in coloured sections of blue, green and pink. The blue section relates to the car specification, the green section has details of the new owner and the pink section is sent to the DVLA in the UK when the car is sold. A small section in yellow deals with selling the car within the motor trade.

Previous ownership records

Due to the introduction of important new legislation on data protection, it is no longer possible to acquire, from the British DVLA, a list of previous owners of a car you own, or are intending to purchase. This scenario will also apply to dealerships and other specialists, who you may wish to make contact with and acquire information on previous ownership and work carried out.

If the car has a foreign registration, there may be expensive and time-consuming formalities to complete. Do you really want the hassle?

Roadworthiness certificate

Most country/state administrations require that vehicles are regularly tested to prove that they are safe to use on the public highway and do not produce excessive emissions. In the UK that test (the 'MOT') is carried out at approved testing stations, for a fee. In the USA the requirement varies, but most states insist on an emissions test every two years as a minimum, while the police are charged with pulling over unsafe-looking vehicles.

In the UK the test is required on an annual basis once a vehicle becomes three years old. Of particular relevance for older cars is that the certificate issued includes the mileage reading recorded at the test date and, therefore, becomes an independent record of that car's history. Ask the seller if previous certificates are

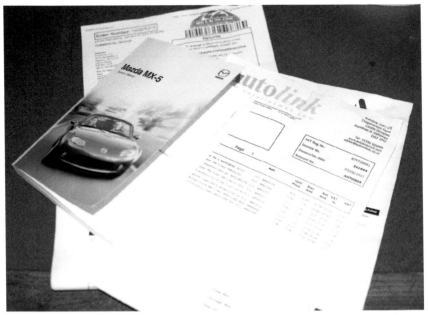

Paperwork covers everything from manuals to receipts. It is all pertinent to the history of the car.

available. Without an MOT the vehicle should be trailered to its new home, unless you insist that a valid MOT is part of the deal. (Not such a bad idea this, as at least you will know the car was roadworthy on the day it was tested and you don't need to wait for the old certificate to expire before having the test done.)

Road licence

The administration of every country/state charges some kind of tax for the use of its road system, the actual form of the 'road licence' and how it is displayed, varying enormously from country to country and state to state.

Whatever the form of the road licence, it must relate to the vehicle carrying it and must be present and valid if the car is to be driven on the public highway legally.

Changed legislation in the UK means that the seller of a car must surrender any existing road fund licence, and it is the responsibility of the new owner to re-tax the vehicle at the time of purchase and before the car can be driven on the road. It's therefore vital to see the Vehicle Registration Certificate (V5C) at the time of purchase, and to have access to the New Keeper Supplement (V5C/2), allowing the buyer to obtain road tax immediately.

In the UK, classic vehicles 40 years old or more on the 1st January each year get free road tax. It is still necessary to renew the tax status every year, even if there is no change.

If the car is untaxed because it has not been used for a period of time, the owner has to inform the licensing authorities.

Certificates of authenticity

For many makes of collectible car it is possible to get a certificate proving the age and authenticity (e.g. engine and chassis numbers, paint colour and trim) of a particular vehicle, these are sometimes called 'Heritage Certificates' and if the car comes with one of these it is a definite bonus. If you want to obtain one, the relevant owners' club is the best starting point.

If the car has been used in European classic car rallies it may have a FIVA (Fédération International des Véhicules Anciens) certificate. The so-called 'FIVA Passport' or 'FIVA Vehicle Identity Card' enables organisers and participants to recognise whether or not a particular vehicle is suitable for individual events. If you want to obtain such a certificate go to www.fbhvc.co.uk or www.fiva.org, there will be similar organisations in other countries too.

Valuation certificate

Hopefully, the vendor will have a recent valuation certificate, or letter signed by a recognised expert stating how much he, or she, believes the particular car to be worth (such documents, together with photos, are usually needed to get 'agreed value' insurance). Generally, such documents should act only as confirmation of your own assessment of the car rather than a guarantee of value as the expert has probably not seen the car in the flesh. The easiest way to find out how to obtain a formal valuation is to contact the owners' club.

Service history

Often, these cars will have been serviced at home by enthusiastic (and hopefully capable) owners for a good number of years. Nevertheless, try to obtain as much service history and other paperwork pertaining to the car as you can. Naturally, dealer stamps, or specialist garage receipts score most points in the value stakes. However, anything helps in the great authenticity game, items like the original bill of sale, handbook, parts invoices and repair bills, adding to the story and the character of the car. Even a brochure correct to the year of the car's manufacture is a useful document and something that you could well have to search hard for to locate in future years. If the seller claims that the car has been restored, then expect receipts and other evidence from a specialist restorer.

If the seller claims to have carried out regular servicing, ask what work was completed, when, and seek some evidence of it being carried out. Your assessment of the car's overall condition should tell you whether the seller's claims are genuine.

Restoration photographs

If the seller tells you that the car has been restored, then expect to be shown a series of photographs taken while the restoration was under way. Pictures taken at various stages, and from various angles, should help you gauge the thoroughness of the work. If you buy the car, ask if you can have all the photographs, as they form an important part of the vehicle's history. It's surprising how many sellers are happy to part with their car and accept your cash, but want to hang on to their photographs! In the latter event, you may be able to persuade the vendor to get a set of copies made.

Condition

If the car you've been looking at is really bad, then you've probably not bothered to use the marking system in chapter 9 – the 60 minute evaluation. You may not have even got as far as using that chapter at all!

If you did use the marking system in chapter 9 you'll know whether the car is in Excellent (maybe Concours), Good, Average or Poor condition or, perhaps, somewhere in-between these categories.

Many car magazines run a regular price guide. If you haven't bought the latest editions, do so now and compare their suggested values for the model you are thinking of buying: also look at the auction prices they're reporting. Values have been fairly stable for some time, but some models will always be more sought-after than others. Trends can change too. The values published in the magazines tend to vary from one magazine to another, as do their scales of condition, so read carefully the guidance notes they provide. Bear in mind that a car that is truly a recent show winner could be worth more than the highest scale published. Assuming that the car you have in mind is not in show/concours condition, then relate the level of condition that you judge the car to be in with the appropriate guide price. How does the figure compare with the asking price? Before you start haggling with the seller, consider what effect any variation from standard specification might have on the car's value.

The **VVT** solenoid (arrowed) is the give-away that this is a 2.0-litre engine. The 1.8-litre does not have this.

Rust is never desirable. Hopefully, the previous chapters have helped you avoid this.

If you are buying from a dealer, remember there will be a dealer's premium on the price.

Desirable options/extras

On soft top cars an optional hardtop is worth having; it is a valuable and relatively rare accessory.

2.0-litre models are generally more valuable than the 1.8s, and special editions are marginally more desirable than standard cars, due to the alternative spec and colour schemes (not to all tastes).

Colours generally balance out in desirability, with no one colour being seen as super desirable or undesirable. Likewise for interiors: while generally leather is appreciated more than cloth, there are buyers who prefer cloth.

Limited-slip differential on the 2.0-litre cars (UK) is a good feature to have.

Air-conditioning on the higher specification cars is desired.

An aftermarket exhaust is a generally desired feature among many owners, as are stereo upgrades.

The later cars are more desirable and therefore cost more, due to a nicer interior, face-lifted exterior and some mechanical improvements.

Among the more desirable models are the Sport models in the earlier NC1, the Z-Sport (if a UK car, or Blaze, as it is known in Japan) which is based on the Sport but comes with the fantastic Radiant Ebony paint colour and BBS wheels, among many other nice styling features. The Venture (NC2) and Sport Venture (NC3) are always popular due to the nice touch-screen satellite navigation and some great colour combinations. In the UK the 20th anniversary model is a lovely example of a special edition based on the 1.8 base model, with great colour choices and a smattering of extras, it was intended to remind us what MX-5s are all about. In Japan, however, it was based on the top specification model with almost every option box ticked. The 25th anniversary car was another winner, painted in the fantastic Soul Red colour, and with a gift in the glovebox in the form of a nice watch from Torneau, in a similar vein to the 10th anniversary Mk2.

In short, all the special editions are great, there isn't a bad one, as the cars they are based on are so good.

This picture shows the bottom end of an engine, the crankshaft, connecting rods and main bearing caps: this is a view you should never have to see. To avoid this, check the car you want to buy carefully using this book, keep your new car serviced, and check the oil level regularly. This will give you years of good service.

Undesirable features
The most undesirable specification is an early basic 1.8-litre car, although it isn't in any way a bad car.

Otherwise, really the most undesirable features will be damage or corrosion that have occurred over the years, a knocking engine if the owner hasn't kept a close eye on oil levels/consumption, or modifications that aren't to everyone's taste, such as excessively loud exhausts, very low suspension, stickers, unusual paint finishes, or even oversized wheels, which can have a detrimental effect on the drive of an MX-5.

The automatic gearbox is worthy of mention here. You would generally expect an automatic sports car to be a fairly undesirable option, however, on the Mk3 the excellent six-speed automatic is enjoyed by many. For those who have no choice but to drive an automatic, it is definitely not an inferior car.

Striking a deal
Negotiate on the basis of your condition assessment, mileage, and fault rectification cost. Also take into account the car's specification. Be realistic about the value, but don't be completely intractable: a small compromise on the part of the vendor or buyer will often facilitate a deal at little real cost.

Restorations are great fun, as an owner who has restored well over 30 classic cars for myself over the years, not to mention dozens more for customers, I would never try to put someone off restoring their dream car. However, it always costs more than you would expect, you always find things wrong once you get into a job, even on the most perfect cars. On a project car these things just add to an already expensive job.

Due to the car's age (at time of writing), it would be unusual to find a Mk3 MX-5 that had been stripped down and is being sold as a project. Chances are such a car would probably have been accident damaged and the advice would be to steer clear, but it's generally advisable to avoid stripped cars, as parts are always missing.

There is a lot to be said for rolling restorations, that is to say a car you can drive while doing bits on it. The advantage here is you get to enjoy the car from day one. Often the thing that kills a restoration is getting sick of working on a car without the fun, so the project stalls. It also means you actually get some use out of the car. If the project fails at least you have had some fun from the car, and likely learnt a lot for the next one; a much better situation than having a lump of metal in the garage that has become a noose around your neck.

If you do go for a full restoration then make sure you know what you are getting yourself into. By this I mean don't let yourself get any nasty surprises; for example, if the car doesn't start because of a minor issue, sort that minor issue and make sure it runs. Can you imagine how soul destroying it would be to restore the bodywork at

Restorations can be a lot of fun ...

... but they are a huge draw on both time and money.

Be very sure – before deciding to take on a restoration project – that you wouldn't rather just start with a nice car, and tweak it, as the owner of this example has done, to make it your own.

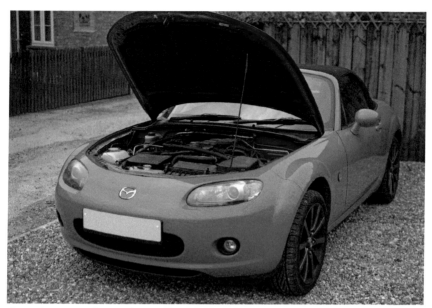

A good compromise can be a rolling restoration. This Mk3 Sport was a cheap scruffy project, which also served as the author's daily driver.

great effort and expense only to find the engine needs rebuilding! It's worth getting the car on a ramp before you start, too – you will see much more and save a lot of heartache, allowing you to plan properly.

Finally make a plan. Do the car in sections, I'd suggest starting with the bodyshell, then move on to the mechanicals, then any trim jobs. As a restorer who buys cars I see a surprising amount of projects (and often buy them) which started full of hope as the owner spent a lot on mechanicals and trim only to realise very quickly the welding was beyond them. These cars make great donors for parts, try to save yourself from going down the same path.

To put it simply, other than the fun of a project, restoring cars only makes sense when it's done for spreading the cost. It is almost always cheaper to buy a good example of the car concerned.

14 Paint problems

– bad complexion, including dimples, pimples and bubbles

Paint faults generally occur due lack of protection/maintenance, or to poor preparation prior to a respray or touch-up. Some of the following conditions may be present in the car you're looking at:

Orange peel

This appears as an uneven paint surface, similar to the appearance of the skin of an orange. The fault is caused by the failure of atomized paint droplets to flow into each other when they hit the surface. It's sometimes possible to rub out the effect with proprietary paint cutting/rubbing compound or very fine grades of abrasive paper. A respray may be necessary in severe cases. Consult a bodywork repairer/paint shop for advice on the particular car.

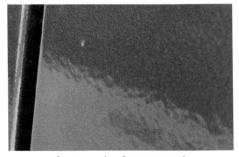

An example of orange peel.

Cracking

Severe cases are likely to have been caused by too heavy an application of paint (or filler beneath the paint). Also, insufficient stirring of the paint before application can lead to the components being improperly mixed, and cracking can result. Incompatibility with the paint already on the panel can have a similar effect. To rectify the problem it is necessary to rub down to a smooth, sound finish before respraying the problem area.

Cracking.

Crazing

Sometimes the paint takes on a crazed rather than a cracked appearance when the problems mentioned under 'Cracking' are present. This problem can also be

An extreme case of crazing can be seen here; the paint is literally peeling away.

caused by a reaction between the underlying surface and the paint. Paint removal and respraying the problem area is usually the only solution.

Blistering

Almost always caused by corrosion of the metal beneath the paint. Usually perforation will be found in the metal and the damage will usually be worse than that suggested by the area of blistering. The metal will have to be repaired before repainting.

Micro blistering

Usually the result of an economy respray where inadequate heating has allowed moisture to settle on the car before spraying. Consult a paint specialist, but usually damaged paint will have to be removed before partial or full respraying. Can also be caused by car covers that don't 'breathe'.

Micro blistering.

Fading

Some colours, especially reds, are prone to fading if subjected to strong sunlight for long periods without the benefit of polish protection. Sometimes proprietary paint restorers and/or paint cutting/ rubbing compounds will retrieve the situation. Often a respray is the only real solution.

Peeling

Often a problem with metallic paintwork when the sealing lacquer becomes damaged and begins to peel off. Poorly applied paint may also peel. The remedy is to strip and start again!

Rubbing compound being used on faded paintwork.

Dimples

Dimples in the paintwork are caused by the residue of polish (particularly silicone types) not being removed properly before respraying. Paint removal and repainting is the only solution.

Dents

Small dents are usually easily cured

Dings and dents.

by the 'Dentmaster,' or equivalent process, that sucks or pushes out the dent (as long as the paint surface is still intact). Companies offering dent removal services usually come to your home: consult your telephone directory.

For some reason Mk3 mirrors are very reactive to paint. Great care is needed not to get this effect.

15 Problems due to lack of use
– just like their owners, MX-5s need exercise!

Cars, like humans, are at their most efficient if they exercise regularly. A run of at least ten miles, once a week, is recommended (for the car!)

Seized components
Of particular note are the brakes. Brakes corrode naturally, but when a car is parked for long periods this can be far worse due to heavy disc corrosion. Moving the car will then cause rapid wear on the pads until the surface is clean, and the disc surface may be pitted, which can further wear down pads at an accelerated rate. Caliper slider pins seize, as do pistons, as well as the handbrake mechanisms from cables to the caliper mechanism. In short, if a car has been stood for a long period, especially if outside, expect to be doing some work to the braking system.

Fluids
Old, acidic oil can corrode bearings. Old or incorrect spec coolant can corrode internal waterways, which can cause core plugs to be pushed out, or even cracks in the block or head. Brake fluid absorbs water from the atmosphere and should be renewed every two to three years. Old fluid with a high water content can cause corrosion and pistons/calipers to seize (freeze), and can cause brake failure when the water turns to vapour inside the caliper as the fluid heats up.

Suspension wear can be tackled bit by bit. Here, tired springs have been replaced with a lowering upgrade kit.

Tyre problems
Tyres that have had the weight of the car on them in a single position for some time develop flat spots, resulting in some (usually temporary) vibration. The tyre walls may have cracks or (blister-type) bulges, meaning new tyres are needed.

Shock absorbers (dampers)
With lack of use, the dampers will lose their elasticity or even seize. Creaking, groaning and stiff suspension are signs of this problem.

Suspension bushes and joints
The suspension contains upwards of 20 bushes and joints. These naturally wear but also age, especially if stood for long periods.

Rubber and plastic
Radiator hoses may have perished and split, possibly resulting in the loss of all coolant. Window and door seals can harden and leak. Gaitors/boots can crack. Wiper blades will harden. Brake flexi hoses will age and the ends can rot.

Electrics
The battery will be of little use if it has not been charged recently.

Exhaust system
Exhaust gas contains a high water content, so exhaust systems corrode very quickly from the inside when the car is not used.

Hood
If the car is a soft top the hood may be very dirty. Clean this before attempting to fold it, or you will grind the dirt deeper into the fabric as it rubs against itself.

A worn steering wheel is simple to replace. You can choose a cruise control equipped original wheel (top right) or a retrimmed unit (top left). The worn standard wheel is seen here at the bottom.

16 The Community
– key people, organisations and companies in the MX-5 world

Most car marques have an active community associated with them, but very few other marques have such an incredibly active and well connected community as that associated with the MX-5.

Clubs & forums
MX-5 Owners' Club UK – www.mx5oc.co.uk

MX5Nutz– www.mx5nutz.com (also on Facebook)

MX-5 MIATA.NET – www.miata.net

NC-Europe.Club – Facebook: NC Mazda MX-5 Mk3s nc-europe.club

Repairers, parts suppliers and manufacturers of parts worldwide
A few suppliers are listed below, these are a good starting point for most enquiries.

Moss
UK/Euro website: www.moss-europe.co.uk
US-based Miata site: www.mossmiata.com.
Moss has existed since 1948 and has been of endless use to car enthusiasts ever since.

The NC can be seen at trackdays up and down the country every weekend.

MX-5 Parts – www.mx5parts.co.uk
A UK-based business which has a good reputation for supplying a very wide range of parts, both original Mazda and aftermarket.

Autolink – www.autolink.co.uk
A UK-based business with very fair pricing, always worth a visit.

Mazda
UK site www.mazda.co.uk
US site www.mazdausa.com
For other territories a simple web search of Mazda will pull up your local site.

There are a few companies who have been around for a long time and produce good quality parts for the MX-5 aftermarket.

IL Motorsport – www.ilmotorsport.de
Produces a good range of both aftermarket repair and replacement items (such as bushes) as well as a lot of upgrade or tuning parts.

Racing Beat – www.racingbeateurope.com
Products are available worldwide through local distributors, but the European distributor is found here.

Powerflex – www.powerflex.co.uk
Manufactures replacement suspension bushes, in particular the front suspension kits are invaluable to Mk3 owners.

Gaz – www.gazcoilovers.com
Produces excellent coilovers for MX-5s including the Mk3, offering well balanced ride and handling. The company is also willing to produce one-offs to a customer's specification, all at a reasonable price.

Other suspension brands to look out for are HSD, along with Meister-r, offers reasonably priced coilover kits which are very popular in the community. Eibach offers spring kits to deliver a sportier ride and lower stance, especially to early Mk3s, without sacrificing handling or comfort.

For those with an interest in driving their car on track, then a roll bar may be of use. UK companies GC Fabrications (www.gcfabrications.co.uk) and TR Lane (www.trlanefabs.co.uk) both produce good solid products and are a good place to start.

It is worth pointing out that the above list is in no way exhaustive, at present in the UK alone there are over 10 well-known, trusted and very capable businesses supplying parts, multiply that worldwide and you could fill the book. This is not a telephone directory though, so the list above is very much intended as a starting point to get a feel for the parts available. Also not listed are any of the excellent smaller businesses maintaining these cars, these businesses are often the best port of call for older models, offering more competitive pricing than a main dealer, and sometimes more experience on older models than a main dealer would have.

17 Vital statistics

– essential data at your fingertips

The statistics below relate to UK specifications, mainly manufacturer provided. However, most of the specifications carry across to other markets. One exception is power outputs, which vary across markets, so you should check your own market just to be certain. Performance figures are also a matter for debate – manufacturer figures are usually quite pessimistic compared to road test figures.

Common specifications

Length	4000mm	(157.5in)	(soft top)
	4020mm	(158.3in)	(PRHT)
Width	720mm	(67.7in)	
Height	1240mm	(48.8in)	(soft top)
	1255mm	(49.4in)	(PRHT)
Wheelbase	2330mm	(91.7in)	
Kerb weight	1110kg	(2450lb)	(soft top)
	1153kg	(2542lb)	(PRHT)

Engine: Four-cylinder, wet sump, 1.8- or 2.0-litre capacity, 16 valves, petrol, made of aluminum alloy.

Transmission: Manual five- and six-speed gearboxes, automatic option (six-speed) with paddle shifters.

Differentials: Open differentials fitted to 1.8 and automatic cars. Limited slip differentials fitted to 2.0 cars (UK market only – in other markets the six-speed manual gearbox is often the defining feature of LSD fitment).

Suspension: Front double wishbone, alloy arms, non replaceable balljoints. Adjustable for camber, caster and toe. Rear suspension multi-link design, with anti-dive and anti-squat characteristics, adjustable for camber and toe. Shock absorbers with coil springs fitted, Bilstein on sports orientated models.

Brakes: Front discs 290x22mm vented, rear discs 280x10mm solid, front and rear calipers single piston sliding, with handbrake function on rear. ABS on all models, split pressure braking system for safety. Cable operated handbrake.

Steering: Rack and pinion operating with hydraulic power steering, 15:1 ratio, 2.6 turns lock-to-lock.

Wheels: A choice of steel 16x6.5in aluminium alloys weighing 6.8kg (15lb) or 17x7in weighing 7.7kg (17lb). NC1 had squarer design wheels than NC2 and 3, but sizes and weights were the same. The NC stud pattern is 5x114.3, and if you fit aftermarket wheels you should aim to be close to the factory 55mm offset.

A note about the steel wheels: they are quite rare, incredibly heavy, and should really only be used if absolutely desired for cosmetic reasons. They blunt the handling substantially, as will all heavy wheels, and unsprung weight is key to an MX-5.

Model specifics

Mk3 1.8

Five-speed manual transmission. MZR L8-DE engine producing 126hp (94kW) and 123lb-ft (167Nm).
Soft top: 0-62mph (0-100km/h): 9.4 seconds. Top speed 121.8mph (196km/h).
PRHT: 0-62mph (0-100km/h): 9.6 seconds. Top speed 124.3mph (200km/h).

Mk3 2.0

Five- or six-speed manual transmission. MZR LF-VE engine producing 167hp (125kW) and 140lb-ft (190Nm).
Soft top: 0-62mph (0-100km/h): 7.9 seconds (manufacturer figure) top speed 130mph (210km/h).
PRHT: 0-62mph (0-100km/h): 8.2 seconds (manufacturer figure) top speed 134mph (215km/h).

Mk3.5 onwards 1.8

Five-speed manual transmission. MZR L8-DE engine producing 124hp (92kW) and 123lb-ft (167Nm).
Soft top: 0-62mph (0-100km/h): 9.4 seconds. Top speed 121.8mph (196km/h).
PRHT: 0-62mph (0-100km/h): 9.6 seconds. Top speed 124.3mph (200km/h).

Mk3.5 onwards 2.0

Five- or six-speed manual transmission, six-speed automatic option available. MZR LF-VE engine producing 167hp (125kW) and 140lb-ft (190Nm).
Soft top: 0-62mph (0-100km/h): 7.9 seconds (manufacturer figure) top speed 130mph (210km/h).
PRHT: 0-62mph (0-100km/h): 8.2 seconds (manufacturer figure) top speed 134mph (215km/h).

Mk3 standard colours

All standard Mk3 colours are listed below. This list covers all models worldwide, so not all will be available in all markets. Solid paints (as the name suggests) are a single plain gloss colour, metallic paints had a metal flake of a single colour mixed in, usually silver, producing a sparkly metallic effect when light hit the paint. The mica paints, however, usually create a subtle colour changing effect when light hits them, due to the mica and pearl in the paint – if, as you move around the car, the paint colour shifts slightly it will be one of the mica colours.

A point to note here is colour matching in the future. The solid and metallic paints are very easy to colour match, however even with a good paint shop, which can produce paint to match the way mica colours work, it relies on a miniature camera being able to capture the light reflected off the surface of the paint. Due to the nature of mica paint this can be very hit and miss. In short mica paint is harder to match than the others.

Reds

A4A True Red Solid
27A Velocity Red Metallic
41V Soul Red Metallic

This stunning **PRHT** model is finished in eye-searing True Red, and has an optional chrome fuel filler. Modification can be a fun element of **MX-5** ownership: make the car your own.

41G Zeal Red Mica
32V Copper Red Mica

Blacks
A3F Brilliant Black Solid
35N Sparkling Black Mica
41W Jet Black Mica
28W Radiant Ebony Mica

Greys/Silvers
42A Meteor Grey Mica
36C Metropolitan Grey Mica
32S Galaxy Grey Mica
39T Dolphin Grey
42S Titanium Flash Mica
38P Aluminium Silver Metallic
30S Moist Silver Metallic
22V Sunlight Silver Metallic

Blues
33Y Icy Blue Metallic
40E Aquatic Blue Mica
27B Winning Blue Metallic
34J Aurora Blue Metallic
35J Stormy Blue Mica
42M Deep Crystal Blue Mica

Greens and yellow
27C Nordic Green Mica
35K Highland Green Mica
36A Spirited Green Metallic
A6Y Sunflower/Competition Yellow Solid

Whites
A5M Marble White Solid
34K Crystal White Pearl Mica

Production numbers
In total there were 231,632 MX-5 Mk3 models produced. From 2005 to 2015. USA and UK were strong markets for the cars, although they were popular in Europe as a whole, Japan was a strong market as would be expected, and, to a lesser extent, Australia, Canada and the rest of the world all bought the Mk3 in good numbers. Fewer Mk3s were produced than the Mk2 (290,123) and substantially fewer than the Mk1 (431,506); this is a reflection on the new car market, however, rather than the car.

Production by year
Year	Number produced
2005	27,275
2006	48,389
2007	37,022
2008	22,886
2009	19,341
2010	20,554
2011	14,995
2012	15,400
2013	11,639
2014	12,246
2015	1885
Years produced	10
Total produced	231,632

VIN decoding
The Vehicle Identification Number or chassis number is the unique number applied to all cars. It will never change, regardless of owners, vanity plates etc, and stays with the car until it is destroyed. Not only is it important to be able to identify the car, it also contains important information about the car in most cases.

UK/European chassis numbers
UK VINs are made up of 17 characters.
The fictional VIN, **JMZNC18F600100001**, can be decoded as follows:
J shows its origin (Japan)
MZ shows Mazda as the manufacturer
NC shows it's a third generation MX-5
18 tells us the body style of rear-wheel drive two-door convertible
F shows this is a 2.0-litre. (A 1.8 would have an 8 here)
6 Transmission type – 2 is five-speed manual, 6 is six-speed manual and 8 is six-speed automatic.
0 The next digit is just a check number and can be ignored
0 Indicates the factory, always a 0, as all MX-5s were built in the Hiroshima plant.
100001 Finally, you have the six-digit body number, this is what marks your car apart from another car with the same spec. These numbers started at 100001 on the NC1 and restarted on 200001 for the NC2.
  So, to take our example, we can see we have a Japanese built (J) Mazda (MZ) Mk3 MX-5 (NC), RWD two-door convertible (18), 2.0 litre (F), six-speed manual (6). Check digit (0), made in Hiroshima (0), first car off the line (100001).

A VIN (vehicle identification number) sticker in the door jamb.

US chassis numbers

US numbers are made up of three sections with a total of 17 characters. Again, using a fictional VIN, **JM1NC2NF1B0123456**, it can be decoded as follows:

The first section is **JM1**:

J Japan (country of manufacture)

M Mazda (manufacturer)

1 Car (vehicle type, as opposed to truck, van etc). This section will always be the same.

The second part, **NC2NF1B0**, is the vehicle descriptor section

NC The vehicle model code, so, in this case, the MX-5 Mk3.

2 The next number identifies the restraint system fitted, 1 without side airbags, or 2 with side airbags.

N This letter/digit tells us the body type and trim, and depends on the year. 2005-2009: '5' referred to a soft top, whereas '6' was a PRHT;

2010: E = soft top, and F = PRHT.

2011-2012: E or G = Soft top, F or H = PRHT, J = soft top sport, K = PRHT sport, L = soft top touring, M = PRHT touring, N = soft top GT, P = PRHT GT or 2011 PRHT SE, R = soft top, S = Special Edition PRHT 2012.

For 2013-2015: E or G = soft top, F or H = PRHT, J = soft top sport, K = PRHT sport, L = soft top club, M = PRHT club, N = soft top GT, P = PRHT GT, R = soft top.

2015: S = 25th Anniversary edition.

(If your car is Canadian then the trims will be slightly different, GX is equivalent to sport, GS is to touring/club but GT is GT.)

F This is the only option for the US, signifying the 2.0 engine.

1 Next up is a check digit, this is not important to us but will be 0-9 or an X.

B The next digit is the important one – the model year. 6 = 2006, 7 = 2007, 8 = 2008, 9 = 2009, A = 2010, B = 2011, C = 2012, D = 2013, E = 2014, F = 2015.

0 Finally the plant where it was made, this will always be a 0 signifying Hiroshima.

123456 – the third section is the vehicle identifier section, the unique code applied to a vehicle.

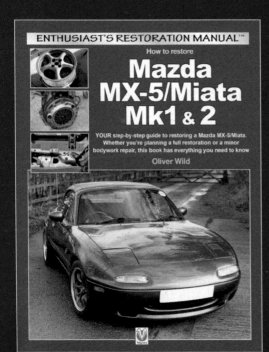

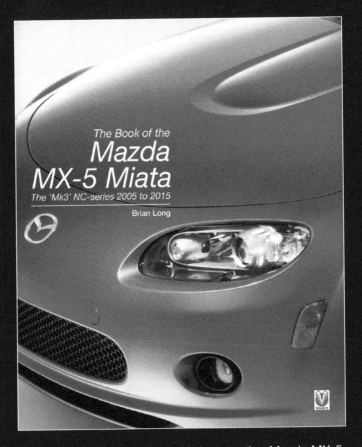